To mme. Kointer·Stace

Fetch –

7/20/09

I hope you don't mind your looks written in, but I couldn't resist an inscription. This book was a source of wonder for me as a child. Every girl needs a little Pete in her life... Tell me what you think!

Ever!
– Catch

From: C.S.E. Cooney

Hawaiian Goddesses

THE
COMMEMORATIVE EDITION

This edition commemorates the national exhibition of the
Hawaiian Goddesses Collection
Fourteen limited edition prints
Exhibited in the Cannon House Rotunda
of our Nation's Capitol
displayed in the Year of Hawaii's Women
September 2–7, 1990

CELEBRATE THE HAWAIIAN

HO OLAKO
We Are Enriched

Hawaiian Goddesses

Photography by Linda Ching
Written by Linda Ching
in collaboration with Bruce Shurley

Photography by Linda Ching
Written by Linda Ching
in collaboration with Bruce Shurley

written under the guidance of
Ho'oulu Richards, Hawaiian Studies Institute
Kamehameha Schools

Special thanks to:
HO'OLAKO; Celebrate the Hawaiian
Thomas Kaulukukui, president
Puanani Kini, publications committee tri-chairman
and
Hawaiian Studies Institute of
Kamehameha Schools
Gordon Pi'ianaia, director

Graphic Art Director: Lorry Kennedy; Williamson and Associates
Logo Artwork: Leo Gonzales, Lorry Kennedy

Library of Congress Catalog Card Number 87-83553

ISBN Hardcover 0-961-989-1-0-6
Softcover 0-961-989-1-1-4

first printing September 1987
second printing July 1990

Hawaiian Goddesses
754 Ilaniwai Street
Honolulu, Hawaii 96813

Printed at Dai Nippon, Tokyo, Japan

for

Madame Pele

CONTENTS

PREFACE

If Pele had never come to the islands of Hawaii,
Hawaii would still be an enchanted place...
but come she did, and with her coming,
left such an imprint upon these islands
that one cannot imagine Hawaii without Pele.

This book is about the goddesses of Hawaii
of which Madame Pele became the most powerful and revered.
It is dedicated to those who still
feel her presence on the Island of Hawaii and
for all who have stood in awe of
Pele's fire flowing down the mountainside,
but mainly, it is for Pele
and her enchanted Island of Hawaii.

$\mathcal{P}$ele always knew that she was different. Even if she
hadn't seen her red hair flowing in the reflection of a
mountain stream, she would still have known that she neither
looked nor acted like other children. Maybe it was her temper, a
temper that was now getting her into trouble with her family.

Pele's mother, Haumea, was the earth mother and goddess
of fertility; her father, Wākea, ruled the sky. She had many
brothers and sisters who were guardians of the elements of
nature. They were all devoted to her, that is, all but one—the
sea goddess Nāmakaokaha'i. It was this sister that would drive
her away from her beloved home in Kahiki and usher her
toward her destiny.

In a corner of a cavern, a child licked the top of a flame. Her small tongue moved faster than the flickering light. Scarlet hair on fire . . . she inhaled the cinders. Flinging her head back, the little girl laughed a woman's laugh.

On the other side of the cavern, Nāmakaokahaʻi witnessed this scene with revulsion. She hissed into the ashen pit and spit out the fire. As the steam rose in the dark, Nāmakaokahaʻi knew that before her was the beginning of a legacy that would burn brighter than fire. From this child, a woman would emerge with power so ominous, she would be called Peleʻai honua—Pele, the earth eater. Nāmakaokahaʻi vowed to intervene with fate.

Then the girl's anger ignited a flame in another part of the cave. Nāmaka hissed again.

"Just a child's game, Nāmaka," Pele said, but when she turned around, the flame was in her eyes.

Just then, Hiʻiaka, the youngest sister, joined them and piped up, "Isn't Pele clever, Nāmaka? She learns faster than the fire keeper can teach. He'll give her the secret of the firestick and knowledge of the underworld flame one day!"

Pele cooled at the sight of Hiʻiaka. She loved to amuse her youngest sister who also had talents of the fire. Like Pele, who was born a flame from the mouth of Haumea, Hiʻiaka was born in an unusual way too—in the form of an egg. Pele had nurtured the egg, and because of this special relationship, Hiʻiaka became known as Hiʻiakaikapoliopele, Hiʻiaka in the heart of Pele.

Pele and Hiʻiaka held each other close as they took one last look at their homeland. Together they would seek a new life far from the wrath of Nāmaka.

*Popoahi. Pele was known
to travel in the form of
a fireball.*

Not long after this, Nāmaka returned from a trip over the seas. She found the land ravaged by fire and recognized the savage art of her sister, Pele. Now she had perfect grounds to have Haumea banish Pele from Kahiki forever. She sneered, "Just more ammunition for me, pretty one . . ." How could Haumea defend her daughter now?
As guardian of the earth, she would have to send Pele away to restore peace and order in the land.

Pele knew it was time for her departure. She thought of her uncertain future as she gathered her favorite things together for the journey. She was pleased that Lonomakua had given her the secret of the firestick and knowledge of the underworld flame to take with her.

Hi'iaka, Pele's dearest, would go along with her too. They held each other close as they took one last look at their homeland before seeking a new life far from the wrath of Nāmaka. Her party would consist of her most loyal attendants which included her brothers, Kāne'āpua, Kānemilohai, Kamakaua, and Kamohoali'i; and her sisters who would all serve her well when they found suitable land to reside in. The group left Kahiki in the sacred canoe. With Kamohoali'i, the god of the sharks, at the helm, Pele felt secure. They followed the stars across the Pacific to a northern fertile land that Pele heard of. It had a rich history and its people worshipped their own gods, but Pele's reputation had already spread across the ocean. When their own fire god, 'Ailā'au caught rumor of Pele's coming, he fled and was never to be heard of again.

They reached the tiny shoal of Mokupapapa. It was desolate but Pele was weary and eager to settle. She brought out her pāoa firestick, struck the earth and opened a deep crater that penetrated down to the volcanic fires of the underworld. "Too small!" she

lamented. Pele realized it would not protect her from the tides of Nāmaka, so she sailed off leaving Kānemilohai behind as sentry.

There were more fruitless attempts on other tiny islands. Kamohoali'i protested, "These islands are not even good enough for birds, much less a home for a goddess. Let's move on."

At last they reached a majestic group of islands to the north of the horizon, and arrived at the island of O'ahu. Her frantic digging to find a home tore craters into the earth and changed the face of these islands forever. On O'ahu with her pāoa, she dug out Pūowaina (Punchbowl), Ulupa'u (Mōkapu'), and Lae'ahi (Diamondhead), but all of these were still too close to her enemy, the water, so she moved on.

Pele turned her attention to massive Haleakalā on Maui. By now, however, the smoke and volcanic glow rising from the new craters that she had formed attracted the attention of Nāmaka. Angered that Pele was extending her domain, she set out to destroy her.

Kānemilohai, still standing guard at Mokupapapa, saw Nāmaka passing his post. "Where are you heading, Nāmaka?" he asked.

"To destroy the fire woman," Nāmaka said.

Kānemilohai sent word of this to Pele.

When the shark god, Kamohoali'i, heard of Nāmaka's advance, he offered his assistance in battle.

Pele stood firm. "This is my battle, Kamohoali'i. I will face my sister one on one."

Nāmaka, however, was not as honorable. She appeared with the sea serpent, Haui, as her ally. Though Pele put up an admirable fight, they overpowered her. Nāmaka tore Pele's body apart and scattered her bones at Kahikinui, Maui.

Nāmaka and her serpent friend triumphantly crossed the ocean, relishing victory. When she passed Kānemilohai and bragged of the conquest, he bade her look towards the channel. The heavens were ablaze over the summit of Mauna Loa and Mauna Kea.

He said, "You've lost, Nāmaka. She is invincible now. That is the spirit of Pele glowing in the heavens. You can't touch her now."

Assuming her human form, Pele had a joyous reunion with her family on Maui. She then turned her attention to Haleakalā. This volcano was too vast to keep her warm, so she gathered the family and sailed to the island of Hawai'i. It was at the end of the island chain and her last chance. They journeyed to the large crater of Kilauea, to a site they named Mokuāweoweo. Pele heard the 'elepaio bird singing and felt this was a favorable omen. She struck the earth a final time.

The fire goddess drew her family near. This site was perfect, small enough to keep her warm but situated far enough from the ocean to keep her safe from Nāmaka. Pele worked the fires and soon had the crater boiling with molten lava which she would delight in sending down to the sea.

There in the pit of Halema'uma'u, under the lake of fire, Pele's family was finally home.

Pele

GODDESS OF VOLCANOES

"Lei of Mauna Loa, beautiful to behold.
The mountain honored by the winds
is known by a peaceful motion.
Calm becomes the whirlwind.
. . . I am alive for your love."

Pele came out of the pit. The air was especially clear as she surveyed the land. Miles of scarlet lehua groves joined the blackened lava plain with the Puna shores. This new land was hers and what she created she would not hesitate to destroy. But not today, for today was a day made for pleasure.

To her sisters Pele called, "Come with me! Let's bathe in the Puna surf and feast on 'ōpihi and squid!" The sisters too were in a festive mood and immediately prepared for the journey.

Along the way, Pele was enchanted by the sight of a native girl, Hōpoe, and her companion, Hāena, dancing by the sea. Pele asked her sisters to reciprocate by offering a dance of their own.

"We don't know this art," they all said with regret.

Hi'iaka, who had fallen behind the group while gathering flowers from the forest that she loved so well, appeared laden with leis she fashioned for her sisters.

Pele called to her, "You're so little, I suppose you don't have a dance for me, but . . .do you have a song?"

Hi'iaka had a bright and endearing way about her. Her smiling face and gentle manner made this girl a favorite among her family. She adorned Pele with a wreath of lehua and then the others. To everyone's surprise, she had not one but two dances of her own composition which she performed joyfully.

Having won Pele's favor with her dance, she left and ran off to spend time with her mentor and friend, Hōpoe.

As the others continued towards the ocean, Pele remained behind with one of the sisters and lay on a smooth plate of lava. "Death to all of you who attempt to wake me from this sleep! Let me wake on my own accord. If for some reason it is imperative that I be awakened, let it be Hi'iaka or my brother Keowahimaka-okaua who do so." Then she wrapped herself in a red robe and fell into a deep, long sleep.

Kilauea, Pele's home

Pele-Honua-Mea
Pele of the red earth

"How strange," thought Hi'iaka when she heard of Pele's request. "The havoc maker sleeps without a bedfellow and chooses me to rouse her. Perhaps it is because she was pleased with my dance."

In her sleep, Pele heard the masterful beating of a distant drum. She was intrigued. She heard male voices, strong and tender, chanting. Pele's spirit left her sleeping body to search for the phantom musicians.

At first the music appeared to be coming from the middle of the ocean, but then it drifted to the direction of Hilo. She followed behind it to Wai'ākea Beach, but then it turned north in the direction of Laupāhoehoe. The elusive drums seemed to move at the same speed as the goddess, pulling her along as though on a string, past Hāmakua and onward until she stood looking across the 'Alenuihāhā channel towards Maui.

"I have chased you this far; I will follow you all the way to Kahiki if need be," she thought.

She flew over the channel to Maui and landed on the hill of Kauiki in Hāna. The drum beat grew louder, but now it had shifted to the western cliffs of Maui. By now, Pele had lost her patience and her temper swelled.

Determination propelled her across the channel from Maui to Moloka'i, then all the way to the northern shores of O'ahu. At Ka'ena Point, she spotted her old grandfather.

"If this is your little game, old man, let this be the last day of your life," she shouted to him.

"Listen for yourself, Pele. The music comes from across the sea," her grandfather replied.

Sure enough, the throbbing music came from the direction of Kauaʻi. She dismissed the old man and plunged into the sea. Swimming furiously, she followed the call to the village of Hāʻena, Kauaʻi.

A few steps took her to the source of the music, a great hall of hula. A massive crowd was gathered from all over the island to attend the performance. They encircled the entertainers and were enchanted by the hypnotic music.

Who was this master of the drum? To find out, Pele's dream spirit manifested itself as a magnificent woman adorned with garlands of lehua blossoms, maile vines, and ferns from the dwelling places of the gods. When she stepped out of the surrounding mist, the crowd gasped in admiration. As she advanced, the crowd parted in awe, creating a pathway leading to Chief Lohi'au, master of the drum.

The goddess lusted for the mortal chief. It would be an easy conquest. When Lohi'au saw the goddess moving toward him, his drum fell silent.

Pele raised her arms and began to chant clear and strong. Her voice had a mysterious power that caught her audience spellbound. Lohi'au listened to her seductive message. Before her performance was over, she had captured his heart. Now the crowd awaited Lohi'au's reply to the stranger but he sat silent, lost in a spell. Pele broke the silence by finishing her chant. Given this moment to recover, Lohi'au gathered himself and invited Pele to sit along side him at the feast. Lohi'au could not eat; his hunger was for the woman beside him. No one suspected Pele's identity. When Lohi'au asked where she came from, she said that she was from Kaua'i.

"I am chief and I know there is no woman of your beauty on this island. Where are you from?"

Pressed, Pele replied, "I am from Puna, the land of the sunrise, Haʻehaʻe, the eastern gate of the sun."

"Until now, I thought the women of my island were beautiful, but compared to you, they are plain."

"You know how to flatter a woman, Lohiʻau."

"I know how to love them better. Will you be convinced?"

After the feast, Lohiʻau escorted Pele to his house. She followed willingly.

In the days and nights that followed, Pele lay in Lohiʻau's embrace but would only grant him kisses and no more. Overwhelmed with desire, he struggled to overcome her resistance but she would not submit. Lohiʻau was confused by the temptress whose behavior made him want her even more.

As morning approached after the third night, Pele said to her love, "I will return to Puna to prepare a house of love for us. When it is ready, I will send a woman to bring you to me. Then for five days and five nights we will fulfill all our desires. After that, you will be free to love another." By now Lohiʻau was crazed with frustration and his passion consumed his reason. In the delirious struggle, he bit the temptress, and with that, Pele vanished into her spirit form.

Because he had not come out of the sleeping house for three days, those who loved Lohi'au were worried. His sister's concern turned to alarm. She cautiously approached the doorway of the house. Her screams and wailing brought the others. The chief's body was cold and lifeless. Thinking he would never see the woman of his desires again, he had tied his malo around his neck and hung himself from the rafters.

The crowd wailed and cursed the strange woman who drove him to do this. Who would do this to their beloved chief? Remembering the woman's extra-ordinary beauty and how she appeared as quickly as she disappeared, they realized that it must have been the goddess of fire.

The spirit of Pele returned home and was hovering above her sleeping body. Her sisters had taken turns standing guard. And now, after days of seeing her motionless and pale, they were afraid that Pele was dead. The fires of Kilauea crater had nearly died from neglect. They must act quickly. They sent a messenger to the shores to bring Hi'iaka back to awaken their beloved.

Hi'iaka

IN THE HEART OF PELE

"...A perfume drunk in with rapture
on the beach of Hā'ena.
In the wind, a premonition,
this vision and dream of the night:
I must be gone by morning:
I travel tomorrow.
Farewell..."

Hi'iaka, lying on the beach in Puna with Hōpoe, was troubled by inner warnings of danger to come. However, she kept her feelings in check. Reigning above all emotions were her overpowering feelings of affection and loyalty for her older sister Pele.

She knew a messenger was on her way before she saw her coming over the horizon. It was her nurse, Pā'uopala'e, whose silhouette shimmered in the sunlight as she approached. The young goddess was moved to voice her premonition in a song to Hōpoe, singing her fears that she would be going away in the morning.

"Hi'iaka, you are so foolish," said Hōpoe. "I can't take your song seriously. Who would send my young friend away?"

The voice of Puna's sea resounds through the echoing hala groves; the lehua trees cast their bloom, look at the dancing girl Hōpoe...

Hōpoe taught Hi'iaka how to make the most fragrant wreaths from their favorite flowers and spent hours teaching her the oldest hulas known.

As if to answer her question, the messenger stood before them and said, "Hi'iaka, your sister wants to see you now."

Around the lava bed, Pele's spirit was hovering about the sleeping body and seemed to be waiting for Hi'iaka's voice to call it back to consciousness.

The sisters were afraid that Pele was dead and were huddled together, wailing and carrying on. Hi'iaka ordered them to stop. "She is not dead. Can't you see there is no deterioration of the body?" She placed herself at her sister's feet saying, "I will call the spirit back." The chant was powerful and it caused Pele to stir. Colors of life returned to her face as she took a deep breath. The fire goddess opened her eyes, sat up and stretched. Then, without mentioning her trip to Kaua'i, she returned to the crater with the family. With one breath, the dying fires of Kilauea crater were rekindled.

Hi'iaka received permission to continue her visit with her friend by the sea. Hōpoe, the native orphan girl, taught her to make the most fragrant wreaths from their favorite flowers. She also spent hours teaching Hi'iaka the oldest hulas known. Thus, the young goddess mastered the most graceful movements of the human form. They both loved surfing the white capped crests and fishing in the coral caves. From a mutual love and respect for things, the friendship blossomed into a bonding sisterhood.

That day while they were riding their surfboards, Hi'iaka had another disturbing premonition.

"My dear Hōpoe, I fear that I must take a long, dangerous journey soon and while I am gone, you will remain here in Puna to await my return. I must go now."

Hōpoe dismissed the idea as nonsense, but as they rolled on to shore, Pele's messenger was there to meet them. "Come with me, Hi'iaka," she said. "Your sister commands it."

"Hi'iaka, you are so foolish," said Hōpoe. "I can't take you seriously, who would send my young friend away?" As if to answer her question, a messenger stood before them and said, "Hi'iaka, your sisters want to see you now."

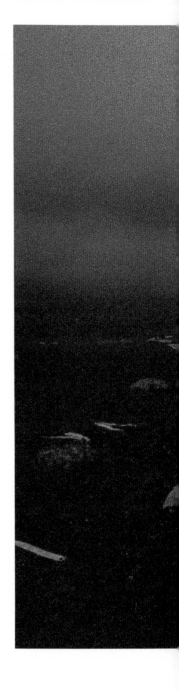

Hi'iaka's dream of devastation

Puna, pelted with a bitter
rain, veiled with a
downpour black
as night. Gone are my
forests of lehua whose
bloom gave the birds
nectar—Yet they were
insured with a promise!

Pele's hearth was smoldering. She had demanded each of the older sisters to bring her dream lover, Lohiʻau, back to her from Hāʻena. Each refused apprehensively. They all knew too well how dangerous that assignment would be. Pele was not offering her divine powers of protection that were needed to accomplish this task. The road to Hāʻena was plagued with evil demons and monstrous pitfalls.

At the time Hiʻiaka had her premonition, Pele had just made up her mind to send the little one on this mission. She was blunt in presenting her request.

"Will you bring our lover. . .yours and mine. . .back to me from Hāʻena? All your cowardly sisters have refused."

Hiʻiaka was true to her upbringing. Without a moment of hesitation she said, "Yes, I will go."

The sisters were appalled that such an innocent young girl be sent on such a hazardous mission. At the same time they felt ashamed for not possessing the same courage as their youngest sister.

"When you return with Lohiʻau," said Pele, "he will belong to me for five days and five nights. When I am through with him, he will belong to you. Listen carefully. . .if you dare touch or kiss him before I lift the tabu, I will kill both of you."

Hiʻiaka got a good night's sleep. At sunrise she climbed out of the crater and saw her sisters crying outside the cave. They begged her not to obey Pele but she mistook their concern for her safety as cowardice and chided them for their disobedience of Pele's command.

Pele came out from the cave and, thinking Hiʻiaka had tarried too long, savagely cried out, "Be gone! You will find no food, shelter, or sisterly love until your deed is done! You have only forty days to return, now go!"

Hiʻiaka, standing up bravely to Pele said, "I will bring back your beloved. But there is one condition I ask of you: While I am gone, you must care for my lehua groves. You may raid the land or destroy the sea, but you must not touch my lehua groves or harm my dear friend Hōpoe."

Pele thought the condition was reasonable, and to hurry Hiʻiaka onward, she consented.

The girl started to go, then turned back saying, "Another request. I need a traveling companion. The way is too long and I need someone to talk to."

Pele appointed Pāʻūopalaʻe to accompany Hiʻiaka, but the family was still not comforted. Pele had not bestowed the young one with mana, the divine power to protect her on the journey.

Hiʻiaka started off once more but hesitated again. Pele became angry and abusive. Finally Kamohoaliʻi, their brother, spoke up in Hiʻiaka's defense.

"She foresees danger and it is her fears that are delaying her departure. Give her the mana she needs to ensure her return."

Pele respected her brother. She decided to call upon the sun, moon, stars, and the heavenly powers to protect Hiʻiaka on her mission to bring Lohiʻau back to her.

Hiʻiaka and her companion travelled down the mountains toward Hilo where they met a woman in the forest. Her name was Wahineʻōmaʻo and she mistook Hiʻiaka for Pele.

"Oh, Pele. Accept this suckling pig as my sacrifice to you." Hiʻiaka liked this woman so she taught her the correct way to approach the fire goddess. With her new knowledge gained from Hiʻiaka, she made her offering to Pele.

Pele accepted it and said, "Did you see some women along the way?"

"Yes, two pretty women."

"Hurry and catch up with them. The younger one is very dear to me. Join them and become her friend and ally." Then almost as an afterthought she said, "If the little one breaks the tabu by making love to the chief, you must promise to tell me."

Wahine'ōma'o agreed and sped to Hi'iaka as fast as she could. When she told Hi'iaka of her promise, the girl laughed at Pele's jealousy. She would be true to her sister.

That night they sheltered at a place called Kuolo on the border of the land of the dreaded cannibals, Pana'ewa. In the morning, they were greeted by a group of friendly girls from Hilo gathering flowers in the forest. Pāpūlehu was their leader and she invited the group to her home where her family honored them with a grand feast. Hi'iaka sat at the head of the table. After dinner she thanked her host and departed, taking Pāpūlehu with her. Now they were four.

There were two routes that could be taken. One was long and winding but safe; the other was through the heart of Pana'ewa, the home of the reptile man who ruled all evil forces in the area above Hilo. It was full of danger but shorter and more direct. Hi'iaka chose to be direct.

"Look there," said Wahine'ōma'o, pointing to a strange scarecrow figure in the middle of the road. "It looks like a deformed tree stump. . ."

Hi'iaka wasn't fooled. She rushed
forward and without a word, struck a
fatal blow. It was one of Pana'ewa's spies
in disguise. With its last breath, it fell to
the ground revealing its true form, an
old hag oozing a slimy excrement of the
most foul odor.

Pāpūlehu was nearly hysterical. As
the others tried to calm her, she begged
them to turn around and save their lives.
Hi'iaka refused to be distracted and
pushed them forward. She was aware of
Pana'ewa's game and knew that there
were spies everywhere disguised in
seemingly innocent natural forms. Every
rock and tree or even a clump of grass
could change into a deadly foe.

At nightfall, Hi'iaka stood watch over
her comrades while they slept. Not
daring to close her eyes, she spent the
night gathering her wits and preparing
herself for the battle she knew would
come in the morning. A bird flitted
overhead and Hi'iaka suspected it was
a spy of the reptile man.

Pana'ewa loved the sweet smell of human flesh. When his bird spies reported seeing a party of four lovely ladies in the forest, he choked on his own venomous drool. He breathed heavily and his eyes rolled back as he considered the tasty possibilities. Then he sent his army of mo'o demons and dragon monsters of the most hideous forms and proportions upon the girls. Hi'iaka fought back valiantly with her lightning pā'ū skirt as they attacked fervently till dark. Dismembered limbs, claws, and chunks of reptile flesh flew through the air, and blood rained on the forest of Pana'ewa.

Pā'ūopala'e and Wahine'ōma'o, who were spiritually fortified by Pele, fought with the same daring as the young goddess. Pāpūlehu, however, was not blessed with protection and fell with the first wave.

It was not a fair fight; Hi'iaka could not see her foes. They were disguised as elements of the woods and attacked at the most unexpected times. She would kill one demon and another would take its place. After a hundred mo'o fell, another hundred appeared.

In the heat of the battle, Hi'iaka, dripping in reptile blood, looked up toward the heavens with a prayer and saw her brother Kamohoali'i with an assembly of gods in the clouds watching over the battlefield.

Kamohoali'i could not bear to see his little sister continue this way. He sent a plea to Pele to allow the gods to assist. Permission granted, the gods forged into battle, sending raging hurricane winds, lightning bolts, hail and pelting rains.

Pana'ewa, who entered the battle as a tree became a victim of his own disguise; he fell shamefully tangled in his own parasitic vines. After the winds tore him limb from limb, he sank into the gulf and perished. His warriors in their forest disguise fell to the same end, as the flood washed the fallen legions out to sea and cleansed the fighting field.

Hi'iaka and her companions watched the victory from a high tree. When the flood receded, they dropped down to the forest floor. Hi'iaka looked to the heavens and saw the gods were still with her, and she continued with new confidence.

Pā'ūopala'e parted with them at Kohala, vowing to join them in Kaua'i. Hi'iaka and Wahine'ōma'o found victory at every turn as they destroyed the demons of each island on their way to Hā'ena, Kaua'i.

In Hā'ena, they discovered that Lohi'au's body was laid to rest in a sepulcher near his home. Hi'iaka was able to restore Lohi'au's spirit to his lifeless body, and with remarkable healing skills, nursed him back to health. Love was budding but Hi'iaka remained true to her pledge to Pele.

On the way back to Kilauea with Lohi'au, Hi'iaka made a solitary climb to the summit of Pōhākea. There she sat reading the signs in the heavens and learned of a great tragedy. Pele, in her impatient rage, could not imagine why Hi'iaka was taking so long to return and believed that she must have broken her vows and dallied with Lohi'au. In her rage she sent a flood of magma over Hi'iaka's lehua grove. The lava rolled down to the Puna sea and entrapped Hōpoe in the torrential waves of hot lava. Hōpoe had placed lehua wreaths, which Hi'iaka loved, on her head and shoulders and accepted her fate, then faced the ocean for the last time and composed her dance of death.

As if for her own amusement, Pele changed Hōpoe into a delicately balanced block of lava which stood on its tip and danced gracefully at the whim of the Puna sea breeze down in Kea'au.

Hi'iaka buried her bitterness and grief and faithfully pursued her mission, but she could not seem to wash away the pain she felt over her sister's broken pledge, especially after she herself had been so devoted. As they reached the crater, she felt an emptiness because now her home was without the two things she cherished most. She sent her two women companions ahead. "Go on and tell Pele that Hi'iaka returns with Lohi'au."

Smoke of Kaliu I thought
my lehua was tabu. The
birds of fire devour
them—Picking at them
until they are gone.

Pele was still crazed with suspicion. She demanded to know why Hi'iaka had taken so long but refused to accept any explanation. What more could she do to hurt the disloyal Hi'iaka? She ordered her sister's two faithful servants to death.

Hi'iaka fashioned three wreaths of crimson lehua blossoms of rare perfection, then sat with Lohi'au on the terrace of the caldera, positioning herself in full view of Pele and her court. She placed one wreath around her own neck and to declare her undying love, put the other two around Lohi'au. She used the wreaths to pull him to her reclining body and put her arms around him saying, "Come closer, Lohi'au. Come closer to me..."

Hi'iaka saw in Lohi'au's eyes that her love was requited and pulled him to her with a kiss. She looked in the direction of her sister and thought, "I'm not the little girl you sent away, Pele. I am Hi'iaka, your dream lover's wife."

She had stirred Lohi'au's heart, and now he could not deny his suppressed passions. Unaware of his audience, he made love to Hi'iaka before the eyes of Pele.

There was chaos at the pit as the sacred tabu was broken. The women of Pele's court were outraged and cried out, "Disgrace!"

The Kiss . . .

*Hi'iaka placed one wreath
around her own neck and
put the other two around
the man she loved. She
used the wreaths to pull
him to her reclining
body...''Come closer,
Lohi'au. Come closer
to me...''*

Hi'iaka was crazed with grief after Pele transformed Lohi'au into a pillar of magma. She tore the earth and tunneled deep into the underworld strata of spirits and death, searching madly for Lohi'au's soul. When she didn't find it, she remained in the black hole for a while.

Pele watched Hiʻiaka's display of defiance. She sat through the performance absolutely calm but the smoldering flames in her eyes gave her away. She was still but everything around her trembled and quaked as molten lava poured out in waves from the ruptured earth. The lake of fire violently boiled over, throwing up balls of flame, and spread over the land.

Hiʻiaka and Lohiʻau embraced in prayer. She was not afraid for herself. The revenge was directed towards Lohiʻau. Pele slowly taunted the man and teased him until he was delirious. The fire woman relished with delight in the sounds of his mortal anguish as she fervently devoured him whole with fire. There was nothing left of Lohiʻau but a pillar of black magma.

Hiʻiaka went crazy with grief. She tore the earth and tunneled deep into the underworld strata of spirits and death. Encountering Wahineʻōmaʻo and Pāʻūopalaʻe on her way down, she restored them to life and sent them back to earth. She began a mad search for Lohiʻau's soul. When she didn't find it, she remained in the black hole for a while. Wahineʻōmaʻo pleaded with her,

"Please Hiʻiaka, get out of this place of death. We will go to Pele. She will bring Lohiʻau back." After a while, Hiʻiaka returned to the pit.

Pele was dark and sullen and sat alone, refusing to speak. Hiʻiaka would not speak to her first. It seemed to her that she could never forgive her sister's unjust rampage. She would go to Kauaʻi to heal and be near Lohiʻau's home.

On her way to Hāʻena, Hiʻiaka was
drawn to the grand hula hall of Peleʻula.
On this evening, an elaborate feast with
games and entertainment was to take
place. The hālau was decorated with
hundreds of torches and the most
fragrant vines and flowers. Music and
dance always soothed her soul. This
would be a wonderful opportunity for
Hiʻiaka to show off her skills and to help
her to forget her troubles. She chose to
play a game of kilu. When it was her
turn to play, she proceeded, as was a rule
of the game, with a song of her own
composition. It was a new song which
she had sung only to a very few. Her
voice was full of sadness as she thought
of Lohiʻau, with whom she had shared
the song so many times. Then a voice
from the crowd joined her in a duet.
Hiʻiaka held her breath, afraid to believe
that she knew the voice. It was indeed
her love, Lohiʻau.

By the divine power of her brother
Kānemilohai, who felt sorry for the
lovers, Lohiʻau had been brought back
to life for the second time. When Pele
learned the truth of Hiʻiaka's dedication,
she realized how cruel and unjust she
had been. She told Lohiʻau that she did
not expect his love and that he would
find a greater love with Hiʻiaka, who
knew how to be kind to mortals. Hiʻiaka
eventually reconciled with her family
and lived happily as Lohiʻau's wife
on Kauaʻi.

In the days ahead, Pele would have
many other lovers to tend to and more
land to build and conquer. No sooner
had she settled in the crater than she saw
the summit of Mauna Kea capped with
snow and marveled at its beauty. She
thought, "Why shouldn't this be
mine too . . . ?"

Poliʻahu

SNOW GODDESS OF MAUNA KEA

There is a kind of strength that is immovable and still. It can quiet the fury of fire and is fearsome. It was this kind of strength that Pele had never encountered before she met Poliʻahu, the snow goddess of Mauna Kea. It was a kind of strength she never learned to tame.

Poli'ahu ruled from her lofty summit above the clouds of the white mountain. She was revered for her power and for her beauty which, they say, equalled the majesty of the snow capped peaks of her home. Poli'ahu kept her domain cold and barren, which was symbolic of the goddess herself, for she was sometimes called by the name, "Cold Heart." However, there was a soft side of Poli'ahu evident of the fertile, sunny eastern cliffs of Hāmakua, which she ruled with love. It was there, where mortals lived, that Poli'ahu trimmed the landscape with ribbons of winding streams and waterfalls that draped down to the sea. She was often seen reclining on the seacliffs of Hāmakua or engaged in sports with mortals.

Poli'ahu and her sister Lilinoe, the goddess of the mists, took off their white snow cloaks and let the golden sun rays chase the blankets of snow up the mountainside. They were on their way to playfully challenge the chiefs to a holua (sled) riding contest down the grassy hills of Hāmakua. It was after a heavy rain, so the course laid out by the chiefs was splendid, thick and grassy.

*Poli'ahu's physical beauty
and power matched the
majesty of the snow-
capped peaks of her
ice palace, towering
thirteen thousand feet
above the sea.*

As the sisters approached the crowd, they could see that only the best were competing on the slippery trail that fell over two hundred yards down the slope. Each athlete had his own holua of dark hard kauila wood with highly polished runners that assured maximum speed. The goddess watched with amusement as the competitors threw themselves headlong on their holua and maneuvered agilely down the hill. Some of the more skilled riders executed the course in a kneeling position. After Poli'ahu watched them, she knew she could beat them all. She was known to be able to execute the slickest course with the utmost grace in standing position.

In the heat of the competition, Poli'ahu noticed a woman in the crowd staring at her with a challenging look. Poli'ahu acknowledged her briefly, then put her mind back into the race. She stood back and watched the others speed down the course in high spirits. When it was her turn, she ran to the top of the hill, hurled over the edge and, with magnificent dexterity, mastered the course and slid to victory.

The crowd cheered with delight and gathered around the goddess with praises and adoration. Again, Poli'ahu noticed the stranger watching her every move. Bothered by this, Poli'ahu whispered, "That beautiful woman in red is jealous of me. I will challenge her to a match and put her to shame."

As she said this, the ground warmed and quaked. When the hot wind brushed against her face, Poli'ahu suddenly knew who the stranger before her was. She had been caught off guard. She staggered backwards, gasping her enemy's name, "Pele..."

*Once on the summit,
Poli'ahu quickly re-
gained her strength
and summoned a
mantle of frost to cover
the mountainside.*

Pele, the fire goddess, was in a fit of jealous rage. She called for the living fire of the deep subterranean caverns of Mauna Kea to arise as volumes of volcanic smoke poured from her mouth. Her hair flew in a fiery mass as she stomped the ground to release a flood of magma from the underworld. The fire fountains burst forth with a thunderous blast, ignited the snow cloak, and chased Poliʻahu up the cliffs to the summit. The snow goddess fled, dragging the singed cloak behind her. Once on the summit, Poliʻahu quickly regained her strength and summoned a mantle of frost to cover the mountainside and blanket the flames. She gathered a massive grey cloud of frozen moisture and wrapped the burning terrain with snow. The cold solidified the rivers of fire and turned the oozing lava masses into stone. Then, Poliʻahu froze the lava streams and forced them back into the depths of Mauna Loa and Kilauea.

The burning rivers that reached the sea were quickly chilled into a rugged land mass. These land masses later were known as Laupāhoehoe and the arch of Onomea. The goddesses kept each other in check. Pele returned to her dominion and continued to rule the southern half of the island while Poliʻahu ruled the northern region.

Ke Kahu Manu I Paliuli
bird guardian of Paliuli

GODDESS OF RAINBOWS

From the heavens, rolling thunder stilled all earthly sounds.
Chief Kahauokapaka recognized the sign.

"A son!" He threw down his fish net and ran towards home.
Like a haunting echo on the heels of the first, crashing thunder
jolted him backwards.

"Two sons?" Arms raised to the gods, the chief of the Ko'olau
ran with his prayers, "Please let it be! Give me a son this time."

*A brilliant rainbow
appeared and followed
Lāʻieikawai wherever
she went. This was the
sign of the girl's great
mana…a rainbow that the
noonday sun would not
burn out nor could the
night conceal.*

As the gods announced
with a thunderous roar, a
second daughter was born
whose beauty echoed her
twin sister's. She was
named Lāʻieikawai.
Her life was entrusted to
her sorceress grand-
mother, Waka.

His wife, Malaekahana, had been forewarned by the kahuna to expect another girl child. She still grieved from the loss of four other daughters that were taken from her at birth because of her husband's mad desire to have the firstborn a son. This time she was prepared. At the first signs of labor, she sent her husband out to fish for ohua palemo on the pretext of having a craving. In his absence, she delivered a beautiful daughter, Lā'ielohelohe, into the safe hands of the kahuna. But as the gods had announced with a thunderous roar, a second daughter was born whose beauty echoed her twin sister's. She was named Lā'ieikawai. Her life was entrusted to her sorceress grandmother, Waka.

The chief arrived, out of breath, at the birthing house only in time to share his wife's false tears.

"The gods did your work for you, my husband. We had two beautiful daughters, but they came into this world without a breath of life."

The kahuna took Lā'ielohelohe to the uplands of Wahiawa and hid her there. Waka took Lā'ieikawai to a secret cavern which could only be entered by diving into a pond at a place called Wai'āpuka on O'ahu. When they arrived at Wai'āpuka, a brilliant rainbow appeared and followed the child wherever she went. This was the sign of the girl's great mana . . . a rainbow that the noonday summer sun would not burn out nor could the night conceal.

Miles away on the island of Kaua'i, Hulumāniani, the great prophet, studied the mysterious sign. After twenty days of contemplation, he was convinced that it pointed to a great ali'i and prepared a voyage to O'ahu for confirmation.

But Waka's powers would not deny her. In her dreams, she received visions of the prophet's pursuit. Suspicious of his intent, she hid Lā'ie further and further as her dreams dictated. It was on these travels that sometimes the girl would be seen and the legend of her phenomenal beauty spread throughout the islands. She became known as Lā'ie, the beautiful.

And so went the prophet's dance with the rainbows; each time he thought he was close, it moved again. Finally, Waka took her granddaughter to Paliuli. Here, between Hilo and Puna, in a secret playground of the ali'i, they would hide until Waka could find a man of the highest sovereignty to marry her precious Lā'ieikawai.

Waka Kupuna Wahine
Grandmother Waka

Miles away, on the island
of Kaua'i, Hulumāniani,
the great prophet, studied
the mysterious rainbow.
After twenty days
of contemplation, he was
convinced that it pointed
to a great ali'i and
prepared a voyage to
O'ahu for confirmation.

Bird guardian to
Lāʻieikawai. Lāʻieikawai
spent her maidenhood in
an idyllic misty forest
clearing protected by her
bird guardians.

To ensure that Lā'ie be worthy of such a divine union, Waka enveloped her in a fine mist to shield her from lesser suitors and stood guard over her prized virginity. Lā'ie spent her maidenhood in a tabu house thatched with precious yellow feathers of the 'ō'ō birds, in an idyllic misty forest clearing protected by her bird guardians.

The prophet, by now, was lost near Laupāhohoe on the island of Hawai'i. Here he prayed, offered sacrifices at the Pāka'alana temple, and remained for a few years waiting for a sign. It was also here that the prophet saw the coming of the chief of Kaua'i, Aiwohikupua. He too was in desperate search of the rainbow goddess, an obsession that began when he met her in his dream. He couldn't see her clearly but the intensity of her aura promised a beauty of unearthly magnitude. He would bring her back to Kaua'i as his prize.

A party of twenty men, riding on the chief's sheer determination to find this beauty, made it through the guards to the forest's clearing. Upon seeing the house of feathers, he stood with a royal cloak of feathers in his hand, the gift for his bride, and all he could feel was humiliation.

"Could it be that my feather cloak cannot even match the fine craftsmanship of the woman's thatched roof?"

Without making himself known to the princess, he left to calculate a new strategy. If the virgin princess had truly been sheltered from men all her life, would she then be more trusting of women? He planned a new kind of seduction and returned, reinforced with his five sisters.

The elder four, the Maile sisters, were
well known for their fragrant charms
and there was no one more charming
than the fifth, Kahalaomapuana, the
youngest and his favorite. The Maile
sisters possessed the gift of sending off
heady perfumes of the maile vines with
powerful hypnotic persuasion.

It was midnight when they reached the clearing. The chief commanded the sisters to prove their worth. One by one the Maile sisters sent out their own particular scent of the maile vine into Lāʻie's chambers. The fragrance stirred Lāʻie's heart but Waka was not fooled and exposed the conspirators.

"This high chief of Kauaʻi seeks your hand in marriage. Take him for your husband," the sisters said.

Lāʻie would not have it. With each sister's attempt, the chief got another refusal.

"Send them away, grandmother. I will not be tricked into marriage."

Mortified by rejection, the chief placed his failure on his sisters and banished them to live in the forest.

"Would you leave me too? Without giving me a chance to woo the princess? I'm guiltless!" Kahalaomapuana challenged.

"Then come home with me."

"Not without my sisters."

He was too annoyed to acquiesce and left thinking only of his injured pride.

The girls took refuge in the hollow of a hala tree. In their despair, they thought that they would be homeless forever. But Lāʻie had not yet encountered the charms of Kahalaomapuana.

Through the fern grotto an odd yet gentle music played with the breeze . . . music delightful enough to capture the heart and imagination of a princess and make her smile. Kahalaomapuana finished her song, tucked the ti leaf trumpet behind her ear, and waited.

Soon enough, a messenger appeared. "The goddess of the rainbows would like to see the little one who plays the amusing music."

Nothing could have prepared Kahalaomapuana for the sight of Lāʻie resting on the wings of her birds, showering her head with the dew of lehua blossoms. She fell to the ground overwhelmed and trembled from the marvelous but unworldly sight.

Lāʻie's gentleness put the girl at ease. "Kahalaomapuana, come live with me as my favored friend and spend your days entertaining me with your music."

When Kahalaomapuana related what happened to her and her sisters, Lāʻie had Waka prepare them a home next to hers. As the devotion between the new friends grew, the sisters pledged their lifelong service to Lāʻie. In return, the goddess granted them guardianship over all the land of Paliuli, with Kahalaomapuana as the royal war chief.

The days ahead would be so blissful in this garden of the gods that no one could foresee the tragedy that was to come.

Waka could not contain her excitement. Through her hidden eye she could see that the new king of the island of Kaua'i had inherited sovereignty over the entire island. To fulfill his parents' last wish, he launched an immense fleet of canoes in search for Lā'ieikawai to rule the land by his side. This, Waka believed, was what would deliver the prophecy of power to her ward, but most importantly, to Waka, it would elevate her own status to chief council and provide her with a secure old age. She maneuvered her players.

In the August morning sunshine, Lā'ie sat with her trusted humpback kahu, waiting to catch a glimpse of the new king. Just as Waka predicted, they appeared over the horizon as though magnetized by the rainbow beyond. Four thousand canoes stretched from shore to as far as she could see . . . leading the way . . . stepping out of the challenging surf . . . she saw her man. She slipped out of sight and sent word to Waka, "Let the nuptial begin."

In her crusty old age, Waka had not forgotten how to entice romance. "Tomorrow at daybreak your young man will surf alone. He can have his first look at you when I send you soaring down on the wings of the birds. This is for his eyes only. All others will be blinded by the Puna mist. When I raise this mist, you will be riding the wave with your chief. Kiss your man for all to see but take a pledge of silence until this moment. When I send the birds and the mist covers the land, take him to your home, submit, and become the woman of Chief Kekalukaluokewā."

Thunder broke through the morning mist...Waka's handiwork...but then another...the meaning of this omen? Lā'ie didn't have time to ask. When the mist cleared...a clue...two men in the surf! How could she recognize her true love? Waka hadn't prepared for this. One of them came for her...she kept her pledge of silence. In graceful union they conquered the crest. She thought, "...he rides like a true ali'i..." She gave him a kiss.

Lā'ie lay waiting on her surfboard with the stranger at her side and watched for Waka's signal for departure. From behind, strong hands gripped the soles of her feet. Virile hands wrapped her waist and held her back from the surf. Her former companion rode the surf alone and landed on the beach.

This other stranger was a tease. "I only surf deep waters, Lā'ieikawai. I will teach you to ride long waves." He carried her out to sea until the shore was out of sightand there were no waves at all. The stranger bowed his head for a minute as if in prayer. She was astonished to see the appearance of the sea god, Kumukahi, stirring the waters and raising the breakers.

The stranger was amused. "This is my surf and the third crest is ours."

Lā'ie was deep under the roller; the crest broke above. When she looked up, the stranger was resting on the tip of the wave with the skill of a god.

"Ah," said Lā'ie, "so this is my husband."

Lā'ie slept in the wedding house in the arms of her first love. This was the start of a brand new life. She smiled in her sleep. Then...slowly...opening her eyes...she saw Waka's twisted face enraged in anger, glaring down at her.

"Do you know who this man is?"

No one had ever yelled at her before, especially not her devoted grandmother. She sputtered, "...my husband of course...Kekalukaluokewā..."

"No, you fool. This is the brother of the sorceress, Malio! This is Halaaniani, who has been lusting for you from afar. Now you've let them trick you! What a shame...what sin!"

Waka vowed never to see Lā'ie again. She stormed out, taking all of her granddaughter's supernatural powers and privileges with her.

Lā'ie sat waiting to catch a glimpse of the new king. Just as Waka predicted, a fleet appeared over the horizon as though magnetized by the rainbow beyond. Four thousand canoes stretched from shore to as far as she could see.

Lā'ie remained true to her husband. They lived as man and wife in the misty forest. It was Kahalaomapuana who comforted her and gave her reassurance that she and her sisters would never go back on their promise to serve her till death. "As we shared your good fortune, so shall we share your trouble."

They were adjusting to this new way of life when Halaaniani's behavior became increasingly peculiar. He invited his wife to join him on a trip to the shores of Kea'au, claiming he was seized with the desire to go surfing. Lā'ie accepted and instructed the sisters to remain, but to look for them if they didn't return in ten days. On the way, he told Lā'ie to go on ahead to the shore; he would like to visit his sister Malio instead. He said, "If I don't join you in three days and three nights, you will know that I am dead; then marry another."

Lā'ie protested but her husband talked fast. When the three days and three nights passed and he did not return, Lā'ie believed he was dead and wailed on the beach. The sisters found her and joined in. Kahalaomapuana noticed that they all cried without tears and interpreted this as a sign that there was no cause to grieve.

"Your husband is not dead," she said. "Stop your wailing and wait a day."

That night each of them had the same dream of Halaaniani's deception and now they believed he wasn't worth their time or tears. The next day they went back to Paliuli to find out if they were correct.

When they arrived home, they heard that Waka, determined to have her way, had brought Lā'ie's twin sister, Lā'ieilohelohe, from O'ahu to deliver her as wife to the king in place of Lā'ieikawai. A crowd had gathered to witness the royal couple fly off on the wings of Waka's birds.

The girls were anxious to see this. Kahalaomapuana summoned a mo'o dragon god and waited amongst the crowd perched on the dragon's tongue.

The king posed, waiting for the arrival of his bride, heard the birds sing . . . the fog rolled in . . . a clap of thunder and the fog lifted. There, riding on the wings of birds was Lā'ie's sister and, next to her, Halaaniani! Again he had employed the black talents of his sister Malio for another cheap conquest.

This time Waka was prepared to over-power Malio. The fog dropped and lifted again; Halaaniani disappeared and the king had taken his rightful place beside his bride.

The crowd cheered and condemned Halaaniani. Waka was still not satisfied. Before the crowd, she denounced Lā'ie, ranting about her granddaughter's "sin." Disgraced, Lā'ie and the sisters flew off on the dragon and left Paliuli forever.

To raise their spirits, they toured the island and eventually met up with the old prophet. He never gave up his devotion to the goddess. He pledged his allegiance and joined the court.

The sisters had a plan to triumph over Waka. They sent Kahalaomapuana to bring their brother, the sun prince, Ka'ōnohiakalā, from the eye of the sun to wed their mistress and restore her honor.

The prophet was lost near Laupāhoehoe on the island of Hawai'i. He prayed, offered sacrifices and remained for a few years waiting for a sign.

Kahalaomapuana traveled in the mouth of the mo'o dragon and made her way to the land which was the pathway to her parents' house in the moon. A spider web led to the house and she climbed it with courage, never stopping to rest. She had been warned of three signs to watch for: in the evening a fine mist and rain that was sent by her father; early next morning, the fragrance of the kiele shrub, the sign of her mother; and by mid-day, the brutal rays of the sun. It was the following evening that she stood at the entrance of her parents' home in the cool shade of the moon. They failed to recognize her, so it was with great wit that she gained audience with her brother.

The sun prince was asleep in the center of the sun's blazing white heat. When he awoke, his eyes flashed like lightning, his body glowed like fresh lava. He consented to his sister's request.

"Look for my signs. After a month of bad weather, you will see me behind the mountain in the shadow of dawn. On the full moon, I will meet my wife. After our vows, I will avenge all who have done her wrong."

Kahalaomapuana was given a rainbow robe for Lā'ie to wear for her future husband's arrival. When she returned to Hawai'i, it had been eleven months and fourteen days since her departure.

*Ka'ōnohiakalā, the sun
prince.*

*Kahalaomapuana climbed
the web which led to her
parents' home on the
moon. Through them she
would find Ka'ōnohi-
akalā and ask him to
marry Lā'ieikawai.*

The sun prince was asleep
in the center of the sun's
blazing white heat. When
he awoke, his eyes flashed
like lightning, his body
glowed like fresh lava.

The prophet envisioned the coming events even before Kahalaomapuana's return and had spread the word. Now, the prince appeared surrounded by a brilliant halo and carried Lāʻie up on a rainbow to the moon to claim her hand in marriage.

Not long after this, the sisters, the prophet, Lāʻie and the prince stood in judgment of Lāʻie's enemies. They stood on a shimmering beam of light extending from the moon, the soles of their feet glowed like fire. The sky opened up and a bolt of lightning struck Waka dead. Chief Aiwohikupua was diminished to a life of a wandering vagrant.

Lāʻie stood at the top of the rainbow ladder extending down to earth. Darkness filled the air and Lāʻie could hear the cry of wailing spirits lamenting the fall of the divine.

Lā'ie put her head into the wooden bowl of knowledge and called the secret words, "Laukupalili, give me the knowledge I seek."

The prince issued a command. "Let Kahalaomapuana govern the land as regent with the aid of her sisters and the great prophet will serve as chief council."

With the state of affairs settled, Lāʻie, endowed with the powers of a goddess, ascended to live in her new home beyond the clouds.

However, it was not Lāʻie's fate to have a happy marriage. For the goddess of the rainbows, a man's love would always be a fleeting fantasy, a mirage out of reach.

It had been a year since her husband was expected home from a trip to the earth and she was troubled. She sneaked into the tabu temple, while her mother-in-law was asleep, to consult the wooden bowl of knowledge. She put her head into it and called the secret words, "Laukupalili, give me the knowledge I seek."

In the bowl she saw her husband had remained on earth and had seduced her sister.

Lāʻie stood beside her in-laws at the top of the rainbow ladder extending down to earth to witness her husband's sentence. Darkness filled the air and Lāʻie could hear the cry of wailing spirits lamenting the fall of the divine. The prince was banished from the upper world and would wander the earth as a ghost until the end of time.

Kahalaomapuana was chosen to take her brother's place in the sun. Lāʻie found it in her heart to forgive her sister and, missing the goodness of life below, requested to be returned to where she was worshipped for her powers as the beautiful Goddess of Twilight.

ACKNOWLEDGEMENTS
Models:
Kau'ilani Alemida
Rebeca Andrade
Jenny Cotton
Simeon Den
Ka'ula Kamahele
Mitchell Kanehailua
Tiara Limoz
Pono Maa
Marie Makamaka
Leimamo Pahia
Lauren Pedersen
Kamalei Sataraka
Sherry Scanlin
Jerome Wallace

Much thanks to: photo assistants;
Manny Habon, Tibor Franyo. Makeup
and styling; Dean Christopher,
Amos Kotomori, Hanalei, Bryan Furer.
Contributors and Advisors;
Thyra Abraham, Winona Beamer,
Stephen Ching, Susan Ching,
Michael Crabbe, Jan Cook, Barbara Hart,
Kaulana Kasparovitch and the
Lehua Dance Company, Milton Goto,
Bill Fong, Jack Faggard, Sheila Davies,
Movie Supply, Gabe and Marlene Ng,
Lynell Totoki, Allen and Joyce Oblow,
Harry Newhart, Randy Spangler,
Ted Sturdivant, Ron Mann, Margie Schnack,
Jim Wilson, Aileen Fong of Trans Atlas Travel;
Audrey Shigeoka, Hilo Hawaii Visitor Industry Association,
and last but not least,
Jose Lee.

Photo credit: MSH, Kapoho eruption
Special thanks to Dr. Terence Barrow,
Pele and Hi'iaka; A Myth from Hawaii
by Nathaniel B. Emerson,
Charles E. Tuttle Co., Inc., Japan, 1978.

Special thanks to the sponsors of the
Hawaiian Goddesses Washington D.C. Exhibit

Hawaii State Commission on the Status of Women
Kapiolani Health Care System
Ko 'Olina Resorts
The Estate of James Campbell/The City of Kapolei

Friends and Contributors:
Dollar Rent A Car
Tim Guard/McCabe, Hamilton, & Renny Co., Ltd.
Jesus Sanchez/Sanchez Bindery

Exhibit Planning and Advisory Board:
John Alves, Chairman
Ed Cassidy
Andrew Poepoe
Jose B. Lee